THE ULTIMATE TOILET ACTIVITY BOOK

THINGS TO ENTERTAIN WHILST TAKING THE STRAIN

I.P FREELY

This book belongs to:

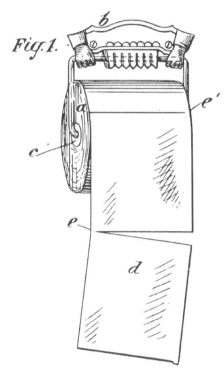

Fig.1.

Use the QR code above to find more great activity books you'll love at
Pink Rhino Press.

If you enjoyed the book, we hope you share the gift of laughter with
friends or family!

Then visit us at www.pinkrhinopress.com to download your free gift!

Gentlemen

Thank you for buying The Ultimate Toilet Activity Book!

For some, going to the toilet is a necessary daily chore with minimal time spent in seated contemplation.

For others, the bathroom is a place of sanctuary, a refuge from screaming kids or the stresses of every day life. And others, well some just like the peace, quiet and relaxation of a regular pants around your ankles sit down!

Whatever your preferred toilet visitation style, this activity book is here to keep you entertained whilst you do your daily business. Full of jokes, things to keep you occupied and trivia you never knew you needed (until now), this book will make your throne time something you look forward to even more!

So sit back, relax... let gravity do the hard work and... don't forget to wiggle your toes if you lose track of time and your feet go numb!

From your contemplation companion,

IP Freely

Ladies

Sudok-poo!

"Some come to sit and think, others just to shit and stink!"

A – Let's start nice and easy, don't push too hard!

					6			
	7	4	3	9	8			1
		8	4		1			
	1			3	5			
8	9	5	1	7	2		3	6
	3	6	8					
		1				9		2
5	6		9	1			8	
	8		2			5	1	4

Fill in the gaps, there should be numbers 1-9 on each line and row to complete!

Newsflash!!!
Astronauts enjoy most expensive poo ever!

Did you know?
NASA recently spent $23.4 million on designing a suction toilet that could be used in the International Space Station!

Its time to go!!!
Help the poo find its way to the loo!

Why did the cop go to the bathroom?

To do his duty!

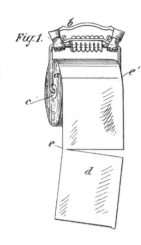

What am I???

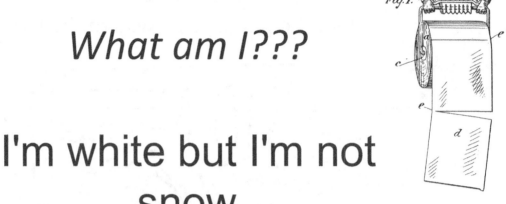

I'm white but I'm not snow

I have a bowl but I don't hold cereal

I have a tank but I'm not in the military

I can be sat on but I'm not a bench

I get flushed but I don't have a red face

It's Toilet Time!!!

Whether you like to lay some cables, drop anchor at poo bay or have to dash to the bathroom because the snake's out of the cave – you can't beat a good toilet euphemism!

From the polite to the inventive… here are some of our favourites.

See how many you can add into casual conversation the next time you're about to drop King Kong's finger:

- Take a leak
- Off to powder my nose
- Spend a penny
- Drop the kids off at the pool
- The turtle head's touching the cloth
- Barbarians at the gate
- Chop a log
- Cook a butt burrito
- Curl some pipe
- Fill the peanut butter jar
- Make a deposit at the porcelain bank
- Do a number 1 (or number 2)
- Make room for lunch
- Release the payload
- Sit on the throne
- Punish the porcelain
- Make like Snoop and 'drop it like it's hot'
- Release the Kraken
- Get something down on paper
- Liberate the brown trout

See if you can name 5 more below:

1. ....
2. ....
3. ....
4. ....
5. ....

KEEP ON ROLLING!

IT TAKES ABOUT 384 TREES TO MAKE THE TOILET PAPER THAT ONE MAN USES IN A LIFETIME

I'M PAPERING WALLS IN THE LOO
AND QUITE FRANKLY I HAVEN'T A CLUE.
FOR THE PATTERNS ALL WRONG,
OR THE PAPER'S TOO LONG,
AND I'M STUCK TO THE TOILET WITH GLUE

THE AVERAGE TOILET ROLL WEIGHS 227 GRAMS WITH EACH SHEET MEASURING 4.5 X 4.5 INCHES!

THE AVERAGE PERSON USES 100 ROLLS OF TOILET PAPER A YEAR (OVER 20,000 SHEETS!)

TURDSEARCH

Are you sitting comfortably? Let's find and circle the poo related words:

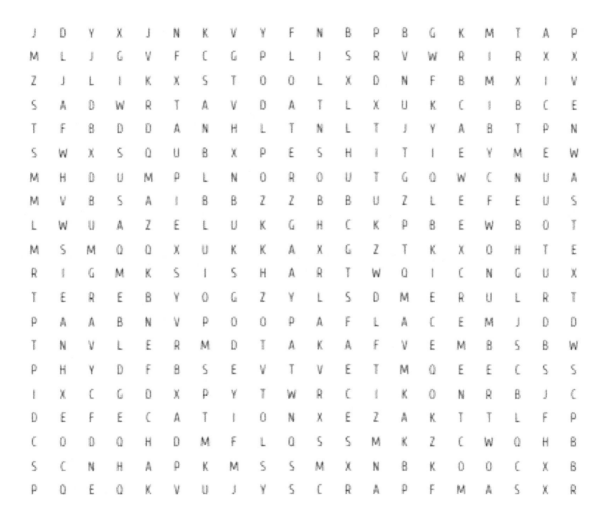

```
J  D  Y  X  J  N  K  V  Y  F  N  B  P  B  G  K  M  T  A  P
M  L  J  G  V  F  C  G  P  L  I  S  R  V  W  R  I  R  X  X
Z  J  L  I  K  X  S  T  O  O  L  X  D  N  F  B  M  X  I  V
S  A  D  W  R  T  A  V  D  A  T  L  X  U  K  C  I  B  C  E
T  F  B  D  O  A  N  H  L  T  N  L  T  J  Y  A  B  T  P  N
S  W  X  S  O  U  B  X  P  E  S  H  I  T  I  E  Y  M  E  W
M  H  D  U  M  P  L  N  O  R  O  U  T  G  O  W  C  N  U  A
M  V  B  S  A  I  B  B  Z  Z  B  B  U  Z  L  E  F  F  E  U  S
L  W  U  A  Z  E  L  U  K  G  H  C  K  P  B  E  W  B  O  T
M  S  M  O  O  X  U  K  K  A  X  G  Z  T  K  X  O  H  T  E
R  I  G  M  K  S  I  S  H  A  R  T  W  O  I  C  N  G  U  X
T  E  R  E  B  Y  O  G  Z  Y  L  S  D  M  E  R  U  L  R  T
P  A  A  B  N  V  P  O  O  P  A  F  L  A  C  E  M  J  D  D
T  N  V  L  E  R  M  D  T  A  K  A  F  V  E  M  B  S  B  W
P  H  Y  D  F  B  S  E  V  T  V  E  T  M  O  E  E  C  S  S
I  X  C  G  O  X  P  Y  T  W  R  C  I  K  O  N  R  B  J  C
D  E  F  E  C  A  T  I  O  N  X  E  Z  A  K  T  T  L  F  P
C  O  D  Q  H  D  M  F  L  O  S  S  M  K  Z  C  W  O  H  B
S  C  N  H  A  P  K  M  S  S  M  X  N  B  K  O  O  C  X  B
P  O  E  O  K  V  U  J  Y  S  C  R  A  P  F  M  A  S  X  R
```

SHIT, WASTE, FAECES, DUMP, STOOL, SHART, FLOATER, DEFECATION, EXCREMENT, NUMBERTWO,
TURD, POOP, CRAP, BUMGRAVY

That's what they said!

Match the quotes and draw a line to the famous person that said them (answers below)!

1. "As he flushed, an unexpected realization hit him. This is the Pope's toilet, he thought. I just took a leak in the Pope's toilet. He had to chuckle. The Holy Throne."

Howard Stern

2. "I will go to the opening of anything, including a toilet seat"

Ewan McGregor

3. "Every time I went on the radio, I would take the crummiest radio station, the station that was like a toilet bowl. I would go on there and build up the ratings, so you couldn't do any worse."

Dan Brown

4. "I loved being in Trainspotting and having to dive into the filthiest toilet in Scotland."

Andy Warhol

HASHI PUZZLE 1

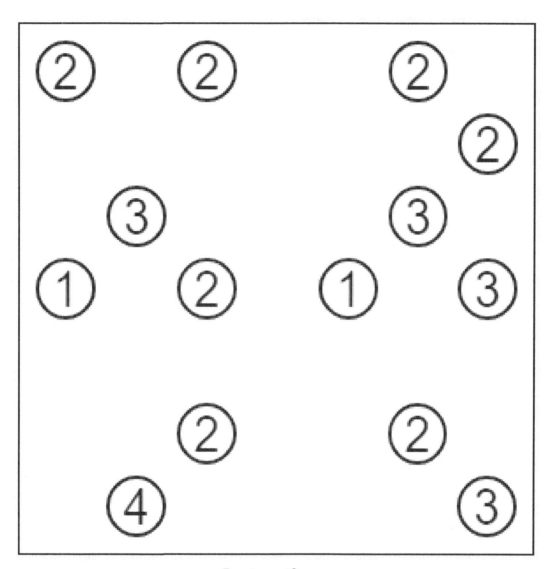

Instructions:

The puzzle is based on a rectangular arrangement of islands where the number in each island tells how many bridges are connected to it. The object of the puzzle is to connect all islands according to the number of bridges so:

•There are no more than two bridges in the same direction.
•Bridges can only be vertical or horizontal and are not allowed to cross islands or other bridges.
•When completed, all bridges are interconnected enabling passage from any island to another

Bathroom anagrams

Take a close look around your humble surroundings. All of the jumbled words below are items you would expect to find in the bathroom – fill in the gaps and see how many points you can get out of 20. Answers on page 59.

1. erotptap lei = ...
2. ugpl = ...
3. aaxrft oerntc = ...
4. tocheau swirnr = ...
5. iidnnefsatct = ...
6. apsmooh = ...
7. oasp = ...
8. knsi = ...
9. cuuerbkbrd = ...
10. nererash ifre = ...
11. woidnw = ...
12. wheros = ...
13. betblb aubh = ...
14. ews aeabtkst = ...
15. tatotpesho = ...
16. sirmsiertou = ...
17. sewotl = ...
18. baht = ...
19. mrrior = ...
20. rtuthbohos = ...

JOIN THE DOTS!

RANDOM FACT:
THE WORLD RECORD FOR THE LONGEST RECORDED
PEE WAS 508 SECONDS (OR ALMOST 8.5 MINUTES.)
WHAT A RELIEF!

The Public Toilet

In life, sometimes the best art and inspiration comes in the most unlikely of places. Doodle, draw or rhyme to your hearts content on the toilet wall. Then take your gems out into the real world.

Did you hear about the ninja that farted?

It was silent.... but deadly!

 # It's Derby Day!

Welcome to The Great Poo Derby, the greatest race of its kind in the world!

Today, it's looking like a two poo race for glory. Who will make it to the big flush first?

Its Bumlog Millionaire versus Redruns for the title. Whose your money on to squelch and slide around the course first? Toss a coin, each time a head comes up move Bumlog forward one pace, and tails move Redruns forward one. Let the best poo win!

Bumlog   Redruns

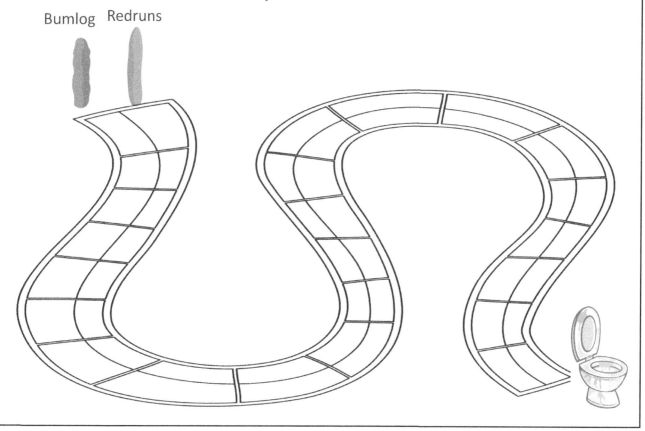

We have a new World Record – Part 1

In 1995, a woman set the world record for the longest human poo at 26 feet in length!

That's the same size as two fully grown adult alligators!!!

Not to be outdone by such heroics, in July 2019 a Belgian man sat on the toilet for 116 consecutive hours to set a new Guinness World Record for the longest time on the loo.

It goes without saying; he probably wishes he would have had this book to keep him company and help pass the time a bit quicker!

Johnny Fartpants!

WHAT ARE GASSY SURFERS AFRAID OF MOST?
A SHART ATTACK!

Is your poo trying to tell you something?

Bristol Stool Chart

Type 1		Separate, hard lumps	Severe constipation
Type 2		Lumpy and sausage like	Mild constipation
Type 3		Sausage shape with cracks in the surface	Normal
Type 4		Like a smooth soft sausage or snake	Normal
Type 5		Soft blobs with clear cut edges	Lacking fibre
Type 6		Mushy consistency with ragged edges	Mild diarrhoea
Type 7		Liquid consistency with no solid pieces	Severe diarrhoea

My partner said she wanted to heat things up in bed. So I farted under the sheets.

The Ultimate Toilet Quiz
One point for each correct question answered.
See overleaf for answers.

1. Who does smellier farts, men or women?

2. What percentage of the world's population doesn't use toilet paper? A: 25% B: 50% or C:75%

3. What is the name of the gas that is primarily responsible for farts smelling?

4. Which British monarch died falling off of the toilet in 1760?

5. How long is the longest recorded pee? A: 820 seconds B: 508 seconds C: 270 seconds

6. In America, during half time of which event see's toilets flushed more than at any other time?

7. How long does the average person spend sat on the toilet in a lifetime?

8. Roughly what proportion of your poo is made up of water?

9. How many times a day does the average person fart? A: 3 B: 15 C: 25

10. World Toilet Day is on which day in November?

The Ultimate Toilet Quiz - answers

1. Women (their farts have a higher concentration of hydrogen sulphide than men, so fart for fart, they're smellier!)

2. C: Around 70-75%

3. Hydrogen sulphide

4. King George 11

5. B: 508 seconds

6. The Superbowl

7. Three years

8. Three quarters or 75%

9. B: 15

10. 19th

TURDSEARCH

Take a break and let gravity do the hard work! Find and circle the different words for the humble loo:

```
N  Z  X  R  F  B  A  C  I  E  X  T  K  G  T  X  M  B  H  V  J
L  O  O  C  I  F  A  K  N  O  E  I  O  F  T  G  O  T  H  U  E
Z  Y  N  L  L  L  J  S  L  P  O  O  E  J  H  S  M  O  H  O  W
T  O  T  A  A  A  H  S  G  M  Y  C  U  Y  U  R  I  C  I  U  A
A  I  V  T  U  C  L  O  A  K  R  O  O  M  N  O  W  M  X  N  T
J  R  M  R  G  T  O  I  L  E  T  J  G  I  D  H  P  R  H  N  E
C  E  P  I  T  G  W  O  D  O  R  F  Z  M  E  O  B  T  R  Y  R
L  P  Y  N  X  M  B  A  T  H  R  O  O  M  R  J  O  R  H  C  C
O  V  P  E  R  M  C  A  V  X  C  P  A  W  B  O  G  O  L  Z  L
T  U  D  R  I  Y  T  O  F  S  R  N  Z  B  O  H  J  L  R  O  O
A  O  C  O  N  C  V  Z  L  O  A  Y  T  Y  X  N  F  F  P  L  S
D  G  H  A  U  H  O  B  T  O  P  F  H  G  S  T  O  R  R  K  E
R  U  J  K  F  J  P  C  O  W  P  E  R  P  J  F  B  X  I  C  T
N  U  N  E  K  W  O  Y  X  B  E  P  O  P  Z  O  E  C  V  L  C
N  K  X  W  E  E  U  G  Z  Z  R  O  N  N  T  O  S  A  Y  F  P
N  V  Y  P  O  E  M  K  G  X  K  A  E  L  A  V  A  T  O  R  Y
M  F  I  L  X  P  X  P  W  T  O  L  R  S  L  I  I  O  T  P  E
Z  J  M  R  W  S  U  H  U  W  N  M  O  P  S  X  N  C  R  O  O
G  O  O  T  O  Y  C  F  S  R  W  T  O  O  G  L  C  Y  Z  A  R
S  C  T  H  S  T  K  K  B  R  O  F  M  U  M  Y  Y  C  T  U  W
B  G  I  I  K  A  C  F  R  O  F  S  Z  V  G  J  N  W  U  P  G
```

WATERCLOSET, THRONEROOM, LATRINE, CLOAKROOM, LAVATORY, JOHN, LOO, PRIVY, BOG, TOILET, DUNNY, CRAPPER, THUNDERBOX, BATHROOM

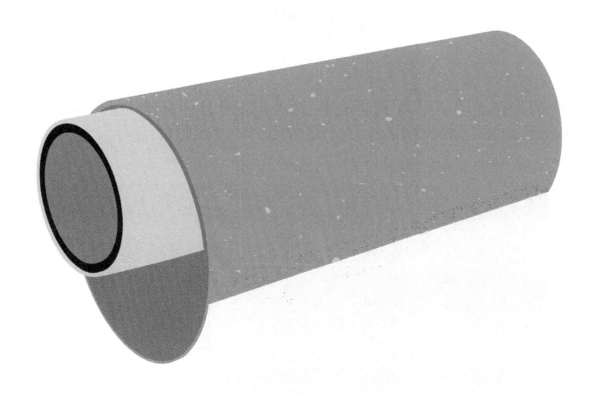

Karma

When you realize that you used the last

roll of toilet paper without replacing it, and are

the next one using the bathroom

JOIN THE DOTS!

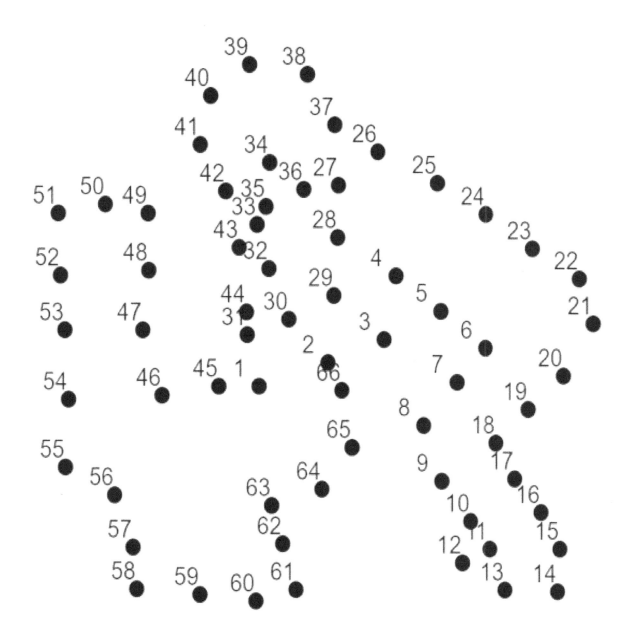

FARTING IN AN ELEVATOR IS PROBABLY THE WORST
THING THAT YOU CAN DO.
IT'S WRONG ON SO MANY LEVELS.

Loo Kakuro!

Fill all empty squares using numbers 1 – 9 so the sum of each horizontal block equals the clue on its left, and the sum of each vertical block equals the clue on its top. No number may be used in the same block more than once.

Kakuro 1

	20 ↓	30 ↓	30 ↓	29 ↓	17 ↓		18 ↓	4 ↓	43 ↓	5 ↓		5 ↓	4 ↓	37 ↓	32 ↓
26 →					4 ↓ / 13 →					37 ↓ / 15 →					
30 →							7 ↓ / 5 →		18 ↓ / 3 →		5 ↓ / 20 →				
34 →				24 ↓ / 37 →								10 ↓ / 9 →			
29 →						15 ↓ / 33 →									
	32 ↓ / 17 →			21 ↓ / 2 →		13 ↓ / 18 →					35 ↓ / 16 →				
18 →			7 ↓ / 42 →										10 →		
4 →		13 ↓	19 ↓ / 31 →						13 ↓ / 13 →			20 ↓ / 1 →			20 ↓
17 →			9 ↓ / 4 →		15 ↓ / 7 →		6 ↓ / 32 →							4 ↓ / 9 →	
26 →						5 ↓ / 5 →		7 →		11 ↓ / 22 →					
39 →									5 ↓ / 11 →					8 ↓ / 4 →	
6 →		3 →			2 →			30 →							

Pay Per Poo (PPP)

What if you actually got paid to poo? A strange and luring concept indeed.

Well the chances are, if you have a job and you regularly head to the toilet to do your business. You probably already do!

Use the following formula to work out how much per year you are being paid to poo!

Multiply your hourly rate x Average length of poo

Example: $20 x 15 mins = (20 x 0.25 of an hour) = $5

Now multiply this number by how many days a week you work, then by how many weeks a year you work.

Example: ($5 per day x 5 days a week) x 48 weeks a year = $1200 a year!

Pay Per Poo Annual Rate = $1200 a year.

Pat yourself on the back sirs and madams, it's a shit job – but someone's got to do it!

Dave has been caught short without any toilet roll
and has GOT TO GO! Help him find his way through
the shop to get to the toilet roll.

Word puzzles

Use the clues in the pictures to guess the well known phrases. Answers below.

1. Paddington Must-haves

2. you just me

3. Injured plus "you twerp"

4. 9pm=$14

5. THI CK TH IN

6. 12 PM / Yippee Laughter HaHa Enjoy!

7. TAKE A PETS

8. (backwards 3)

9. oLD

10. 007 (in wine glass)

11. Monday ⑦ / ② Friday / Sunday ④

12. GOOD

FART WARS!

(NEVER LOSE A BATTLE OF DENIAL AGAINST A CHILD AGAIN)

He who rued it,
brewed it

He who reported it,
exported it

Whoever smelt it
dealt it

Whoever knew it,
blew it

Whoever denied it,
supplied it

He who exposed it,
composed it

Whoever deduced
it, produced it

Whoever decoyed it,
deployed it

Whoever did the
rhyme, did the
crime

Whoever expressed
it, compressed it

Whoever perceived
it, conceived it

He who unearthed
it, birthed it

He who quipped it,
ripped it

The 4pm on Friday poo

The Shartist

The porcelain prayer

The brown bomber

Floater in the pool

You're the lifeguard on duty and the unthinkable has happened! Reports have come in that some unintended gifts have been left in the pool.

Evacuate the kids discretely and count the number of poos in and around the pool so these can be dealt with quickly before the whole pool is shutdown!

Sudok-poo!

"Life is like toilet paper, you're either on a roll or taking shit from somebody!"

B: Medium - It's getting harder, take the strain!

		7	8					4
5			1		9			
4	3							5
	1	8			5		6	
			2		7	4		1
				6				2
	6				4			
9			3			1		
				9			4	7

Fill in the gaps, there should be numbers 1-9 on each line and row to complete!

WHY DID THE FLY MOVE FROM THE TOILET SEAT?

BECAUSE IT GOT PISSED OFF!

HASHI PUZZLE 2

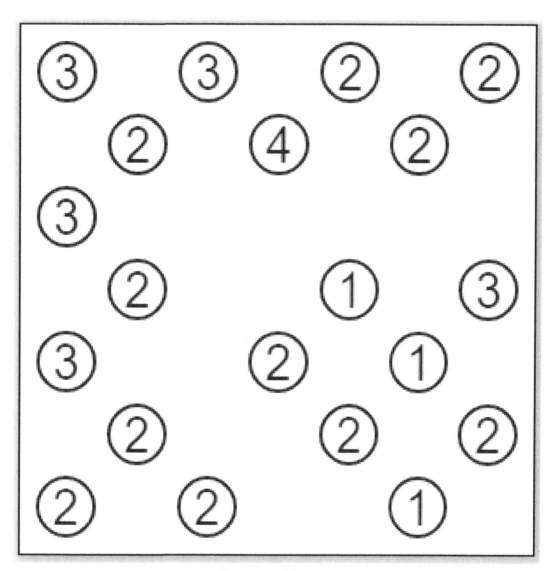

Instructions:

The puzzle is based on a rectangular arrangement of islands where the number in each island tells how many bridges are connected to it. The object of the puzzle is to connect all islands according to the number of bridges so:

•There are no more than two bridges in the same direction.
•Bridges can only be vertical or horizontal and are not allowed to cross islands or other bridges.
•When completed, all bridges are interconnected enabling passage from any island to another

Don't beam me up Scotty I'm having a Shi

Diagnosis Turder

Diagnose your poo from the list below:

The Ghost Poo	A satisfying poo in which there is nothing to wipe after the job is completed. A job well done indeed.
The Floater	A poo that just will not leave. Floats on the surface and often returns after you flush. Like an unwelcome guest that doesn't take the hint.
The Shart AKA The Wet One	The poo that just wont quit. You wipe 100 times but there's still more to wipe. Often pre-emptive of unruly skid marks.
The False Alarm	You sit down ready for action, but the only thing that arrives are a series of loud farts.
The Disappointment Poo	Despite pushing and straining for what feels like a lifetime, the only thing you are greeted with in the toilet bowl are a couple of imitation cocoa puffs.
The Hand Grenade	With only 5 seconds before you blow, this is the one that catches you by surprise and makes you sprint to the toilet. Upon arrival you may need to drop and pop before you've relaxed into a comfortable seated position.
The Second Wave	Think you're finished? Think again! Commonly occurs when you've wiped and flushed before the realisation you have more to give. Often presents itself alongside hangovers after heavy nights of merriment.
The Lincoln Logger	A delivery so large, it may need breaking up before flushing. Can provide an unexpected source of satisfaction and wonderment.
The Cowboy	You've got to get this bronco out so bad, you have to wriggle and buck until the beast has been released.
The Gatling Gun	The one that fires little pellets out at high velocity like a machine gun.

The beloved panda.
They may not be very good at breeding, but they sure do like to fart.

Doodle and color in the panda and his bottom burp to bring them to life!

RIDDLE ME THIS...

1. What gets wet while drying?

2. What can you catch but not throw?

3. What time is it when an elephant sits on the fence?

4. What has legs but does not walk?

5. What travels around the world without leaving a corner?

6. What has a bottom at the top?

7. When is a door no longer a door?

8. What belongs to you, but everyone else uses it?

9. What's heavier a ton of bricks or a ton of feathers?

10. What can fill a room but takes no space?

11. What has to be broken before you can use it?

12. What goes up, but never comes down?

(SEE OVERLEAF FOR ANSWERS)

RIDDLE ME THIS...
ANSWERS

1. A towel

2. A cold

3. Time to get a new fence

4. A chair

5. A stamp

6. Legs

7. When its ajar

8. Your name

9. They are both the same

10. Light

11. An egg

12. Your age

Scientists warn farts can prove dangerous in space due to the introduction of flammable gases (such as methane and hydrogen) into a small pressurised area.

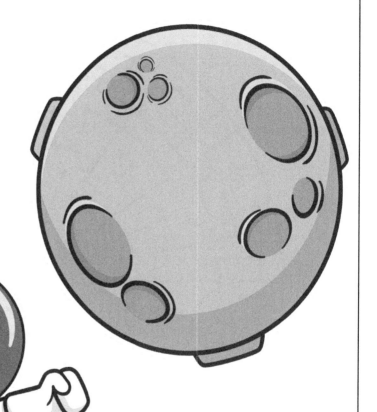

Astronauts agree that the issue is about as funny as a fart in a space suit.

Uh-oh! Nature calls and the toilet is closed. Find your way to the nearest toilet fast to avoid an unfortunate accident!

I ran out of toilet paper so started using lettuce leaves.

Today was the tip of the iceberg.

The (almost) Oscars

Here's one for the film buffs. Replace one word in the title of a well known film with the word 'poop' to completely change the storyline of the film.

Then get ready to write that Oscar speech!

1...

2...

3...

4...

5...

6...

7...

8...

9...

10..

Loo Kakuro!

Fill all empty squares using numbers 1 – 9 so the sum of each horizontal block equals the clue on its left, and the sum of each vertical block equals the clue on its top. No number may be used in the same block more than once.

Kakuro 2

	40 ↓	22 ↓	24 ↓	37 ↓	9 ↓	16 ↓		5 ↓	15 ↓	13 ↓	22 ↓	17 ↓	14 ↓	23 ↓	22 ↓
30 →							13 ↓ / 37 →								
39 →								16 ↓ / 37 →							
18 →					23 ↓ / 30 →						11 ↓ / 11 →				
26 →						16 ↓ / 23 →							7 ↓ / 9 →		
32 →							3 ↓ / 3 →		27 ↓	19 →					4 ↓
4 →		18 ↓	18 ↓ / 12 →					2 →		4 ↓	24 ↓	18 ↓ / 2 →		23 ↓ / 4 →	
34 →							21 ↓	2 ↓ / 29 →							18 ↓
	19 ↓ / 8 →			44 →									14 ↓ / 11 →		
14 →				5 ↓	11 ↓	1 ↓ / 5 →		12 ↓ / 4 →		14 ↓ / 31 →					
9 →			6 ↓ / 33 →									5 ↓ / 19 →			
22 →						25 →							6 →		

WHY DIDN'T THE TOILET ROLL MAKE IT ACROSS THE ROAD?
BECAUSE IT GOT STUCK IN THE CRACK.

HUMOUR

Why did the toilet roll down the hill?

To get to the bottom.

Someone stole my toilet and the police have nothing to go on.

Have you seen the film Constipation?

No, because it hasn't come out yet.

Did you hear about the constipated mathematician? He worked it out with a pencil.

Why can't you hear a psychiatrist go to the toilet? Because the 'p' is silent.

Ya mama so ugly, she went to the bathroom and scared the shit out of the toilet!

Why is there no toilet paper at KFC? Because it's finger lickin good!

Why is everybody panic buying toilet roll because of the corona virus? When someone coughs everyone shits their pants.

Why was the sand wet? Because the sea wee'd.

What did the poo say to the fart? You blow me away.

Bathroom Crossword

ACROSS

3 Clean the gaps before you brush
6 Can force urgency to get to the toilet, not solid
9 Gas, solid or liquid. I'm flushed
11 Open me before the room gets smelly
13 Useful bathroom tool, disperse what's left behind
14 Gets rid of stubble
15 Comes in 4.5" squares, Check availability before doing business
16 Calm and still without me, but white and bubbly with
19 Slang for a wee in number form
20 Reverse of gulp. Holds water

DOWN

1 Replenish after dryness
2 Used to bathe, not a bath
4 Wash with me
5 On the wall, who is the fairest of them all
7 I get wetter as I dry
8 Type 1 stool chart, struggling to go
10 The king also sits on one
12 Australian for loo, sounds like funny
17 Never trust a fart, combination of shit and fart
18 Turn me on for a relaxing soak

I got in touch with my inner self today.
It's the last time I use single ply toilet roll.

AHHH...... PUSH SHIT

PUSH SHIT REAL GOOD

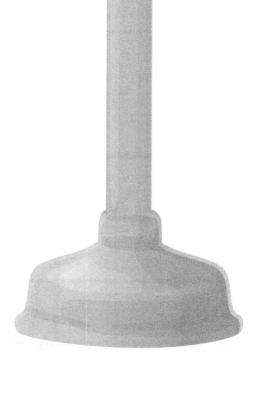

Sudok-poo!

"FARTS ARE LIKE CHILDREN. YOU LIKE YOUR OWN, BUT CAN'T STAND OTHER PEOPLES!"

C – You've got the sweats now, this one might take some time!

4				7				
			5			1	8	
					1			7
					5	8	3	
		2		1		4		
9	8		6	2				1
8					7			
			1	6	4			
2	3	1				6		

Fill in the gaps, there should be numbers 1-9 on each line and row to complete!

We have a new World Record – Part 2

The fastest motorized toilet is the HAWC (Highly Advanced Water Closet) MK1 which reached a speed of 70.5mph (113.5 km/hr)!

The most toilet rolls balanced on someone's head is 101 and was achieved on 8 May 2021. Definitely something to practice during those quieter moment in the bathroom!

A brief history of the toilet..

We may think of the toilet as a relatively modern invention, but it 'turns out' that cultures as far back as 3,000 BC were flushing their business away with their own improvised systems.

Many sources suggest that ancient Crete's King Minos in 18th century BC had the first flushing toilet. Whilst in ancient India, the Harrapa civilisation had toilets in their homes that drained into underground clay chambers.

A few thousand years later, and the Romans made big strides in sewer systems and flushing away their waste. Huge aqueducts brought fresh water into Roman cities, with Rome's famous public baths offering urinal style toilets that drained away into their state of the art sewage systems.

What did the Romans do for us? Well, despite the fantastic systems that were introduced during their rule, once the Roman Empire fell — so did the idea of public sanitation.

Back into the dark ages civilisation went, with the traditional chamber pot returning for many centuries thereafter. Imagine the stench in cities such as London and Paris and worst of all, the unexpected dangers for passers by of sudden disposals as chamber pots were emptied into the streets!

Finally in 1596, John Harrington published a manual for the assembly of a simple flush toilet using the basic components of a mechanical valve and tank of water that are still found today in our modern loos.

Small improvements were made thereafter, such as the idea of a constant pool of water by Alexander Cummings in 1775 to prevent bad smells. Further refinements were made and later in the 19th century, the English plumber Thomas Crapper (nicknaming the toilet from then on!) popularized the private flushing toilet across Europe — leading many to believe he'd invented it.

Fast forward another 150 years or so, with the only minor changes to the main design consisting of the water tank becoming integrated into the seat. Plus the addition of this fine book to help while away your time whilst using it of course.

Cross your legs and count the icons!
How many of each are there?
See overleaf for answers.

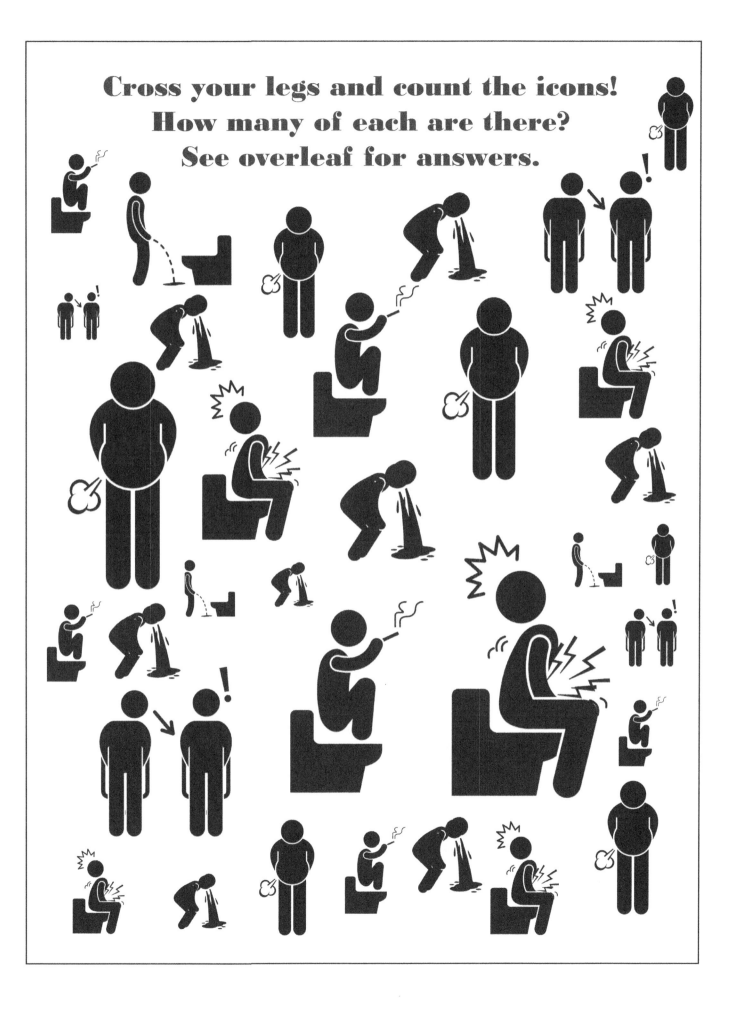

Answers:

 3

 4

 6

 7

 5

 8

FINISH THE DRAWING

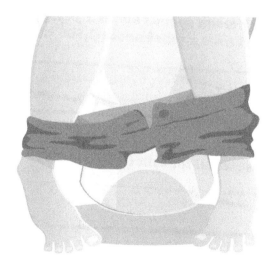

TOILET TRIVIA

Studies show that the time spent on the toilet is in direct proportion to the number of features on the users smartphone

Only 80% of people wash their hands after using the toilet, and only 30% of those who do wash choose to use soap

Although it's difficult to pinpoint the inventor of the modern toilet, the Englishman Alexander Cumming secured the first patent for a flushing toilet in 1775

The average person spends about 3 years of their life on the toilet, and uses a toilet about 2,500 times every year

The Scot Paper Company became the first manufacturer to use a roll for toilet paper in 1890

More people in the world have mobile phones than toilets

Caption Competition

Fill in the speech bubbles to complete the bathroom conversation!

HASHI PUZZLE 3

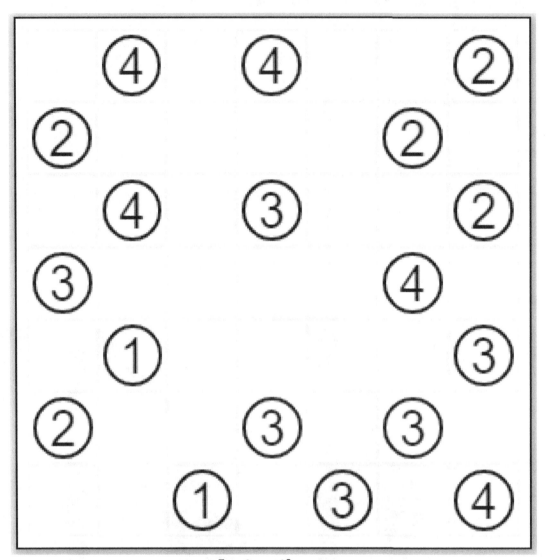

Instructions:

The puzzle is based on a rectangular arrangement of islands where the number in each island tells how many bridges are connected to it. The object of the puzzle is to connect all islands according to the number of bridges so:

•There are no more than two bridges in the same direction.
•Bridges can only be vertical or horizontal and are not allowed to cross islands or other bridges.
•When completed, all bridges are interconnected enabling passage from any island to another

The Great Fibre Provider!

Fibre helps to prevent or relieve constipation.

Dietary fibre increases the weight and size of your poo, and also softens it. Making it easier to go!

Daily recommended fibre intake:

Women – at least 21-25 grams a day
Men – At least 30-38 grams a day

Constipation

Some people say that leafy greens are the best thing for colon health.

But I think fibre makes a solid number two!

15 Healthy foods to help you poo!

- Apples
- Prunes
- Kiwi
- Flax seeds
- Pears
- Beans
- Rhubarb
- Artichokes
- Kefir
- Figs
- Sweet potatoes
- Lentils
- Chia seeds
- Avocados
- Oat bran

'Healthy poo, healthy you'
(Not to be mistaken for actual medical advice)

WELCOME TO THE RESTROOM

HERE I SIT BROKEN HEARTED, TRIED TO POO BUT ONLY FARTED

Puzzle Answer Page

Page.5

Page.28

Page.42

A – page 3

1	2	9	7	5	6	3	4	8
6	7	4	3	9	8	2	5	1
3	5	8	4	2	1	6	9	7
4	1	7	6	3	5	8	2	9
8	9	5	1	7	2	4	3	6
2	3	6	8	4	9	1	7	5
7	4	1	5	8	3	9	6	2
5	6	2	9	1	4	7	8	3
9	8	3	2	6	7	5	1	4

B - page 33

1	2	7	8	5	3	6	9	4
5	8	6	1	4	9	2	7	3
4	3	9	7	2	6	8	1	5
2	1	8	4	3	5	7	6	9
6	9	5	2	8	7	4	3	1
3	7	4	9	6	1	5	8	2
7	6	3	5	1	4	9	2	8
9	4	2	3	7	8	1	5	6
8	5	1	6	9	2	3	4	7

Anagrams - page 13

Anagram answers:

1. Toilet paper
2. Plug
3. Extractor fan
4. Shower curtain
5. Disinfectant
6. Shampoo
7. Soap
8. Sink
9. Rubber duck
10. Air freshener
11. Window
12. Shower
13. Bubble bath
14. Waste basket
15. Toothpaste
16. Moisturiser
17. Towels
18. Bath
19. Mirror
20. Toothbrush

C – page 48

4	1	8	9	7	2	5	6	3
7	2	3	5	4	6	1	8	9
6	9	5	3	8	1	2	4	7
1	6	7	4	9	5	8	3	2
3	5	2	7	1	8	4	9	6
9	8	4	6	2	3	7	5	1
8	4	6	2	3	7	9	1	5
5	7	9	1	6	4	3	2	8
2	3	1	8	5	9	6	7	4

Puzzle Answer Page 2

Kikuro 1 - page 26

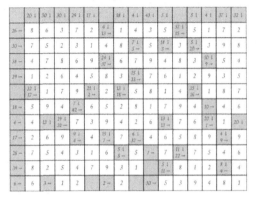

Kikuro 2 - page 44

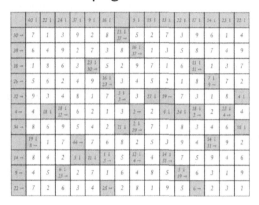

Crossword - page 46

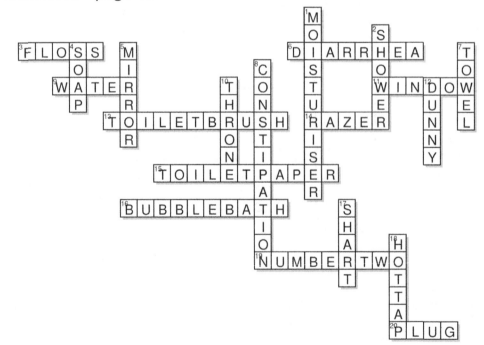

Puzzle Answer Page 3

Hashi 1 - page 11

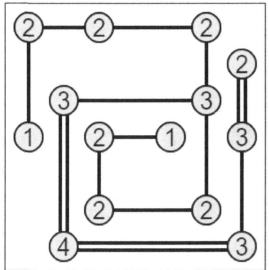

Hashi 2 - page 35

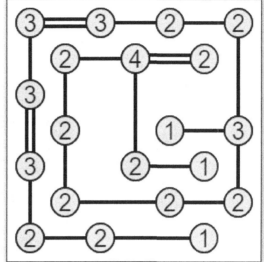

Hashi 3 - page 56

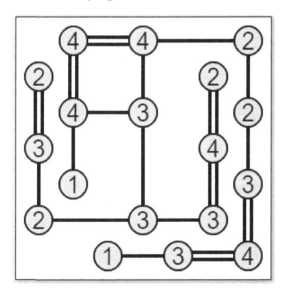

The Ultimate Bedroom Activity Book

If you enjoyed this awesome collection of toilet themed gags and entertainment, we think you'll love Ivana Humpalot's book full of bedroom themed fun.
The perfect gift for lovers, couples, friends and family!

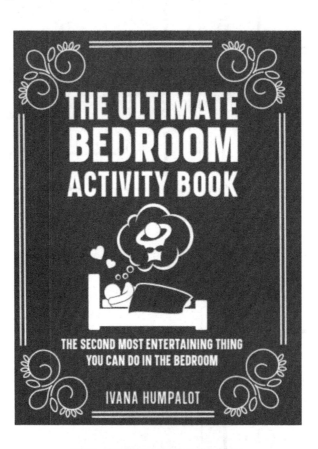

Just use the QR code above to take you straight to the book!

Thank you!

Just a note to say thank you for buying this book from us at Pink Rhino Press. We hope you love reading it as much as we loved creating it!

If you enjoyed our book, please consider leaving us a review on Amazon to help us keep creating more books that you'll love.

You can also:

- **Check out our other books by scanning the QR code below**

  - **Follow the Pink Rhino Press profile on Amazon**

www.pinkrhinopress.com

Made in the USA
Las Vegas, NV
29 October 2023

79882045R00037